Narcissism

A Comprehensive Guide To Stop Being Egotistical, Abusive, And Controlling

(Steps To Comprehend And Overcome Maternal Narcissism)

Hans-Georg Appel

TABLE OF CONTENT

chapter 1: How To Recover From A Narcissistic Relationship 1

Chapter 2: Clarify And Set Your Own Boundaries. 7

Chapter 3: Acknowledge Your Irritation When Dealing With Narcissism. 8

Chapter 4: Several Types Of Narcissists 14

Chapter 5: How To Address Narcissistic Personality Disorder 21

Chapter 6: Type-Casting The Darkness 26

Chapter 7: Cognitive Dissonance 32

Chapter 8: My Partner May Be A Narcissist. 39

Chapter 9: They Gain From Your Compliments. 43

Chapter 10: What Is A Narcissistic Abuse Cycle & How Does It Work 45

Chapter 11: Sexuality And Narcissism In The Shadows 59

Chapter 12: Can Narcissistic Individuals "Catch" Yawns? 72

Chapter 13: This Behavior Stems From Their Own Insecurities. 74

Chapter 1: How To Recover From A Narcissistic Relationship

You may be a victim of narcissistic abuse if you exhibit any of the following warning signs. A narcissistic spouse may appear perfect at the beginning of a romantic relationship, but as time passes, their behavior patterns change and they begin to employ manipulative tactics. Other indicators include feeling confused, angry, or guilty about events that were not your fault and for which you are compelled to accept responsibility. Embedded public humiliation that masquerades as humor may be a component of narcissistic abuse. However, the damage caused by narcissistic abuse is repairable.

Lack of a realistic worldview is one of the defining characteristics of narcissistic personality disorder. In the narcissist's self-centered worldview, they are the centre of attention, and everyone else exists solely to support and sustain them. Attracted individuals are dazzled by the narcissist's phoney self-assurance, persuasive arguments, endearing demeanour, and astounding persistence. In exchange for interpersonal harmony, non-narcissists frequently sacrifice their own principles, morals, and ideals.

However, this is where the basis for disruption is established. Non-narcissists are oblivious to the fact that their pursuit of tranquilly is actually a gradual erosion of their personality. The distorted narcissist perspective now permeates nearly every aspect of an individual's life as they become interdependent. New standards have been established for how to dress, how to behave, who to associate with, when and where one should interact. The non-perception narcissist's of the truth becomes increasingly hazy as they strictly adhere to the rules.

The narcissist assumes sole responsibility for life filtering. The haze reduces a person's ability to detect extreme threats, leaving them vulnerable to future assaults. They choose a stressful environment rife with anxiety over failing the narcissist, who regrettably believes that this is how life should be. It is therefore understandable why the non-narcissist experiences pain when the relationship ends.

If you just ended a violent relationship with a narcissist, you are likely experiencing a great deal of pain and bewilderment. Even if you sincerely believe you were not at fault, acknowledging this is always a different matter. Your mental anguish may increase as you contemplate what you could have done differently to prevent the abuse or assist your loved one in resolving their problems. These variables may impact your capacity to heal.

You recognise that the relationship was unhealthy. You are aware that they mistreated you. However, you still recall the pleasant moments you shared and how you initially felt. These memories may fuel your desire for their company and your desire to do anything to win their affection and approval once more.

Abuse frequently causes severe trauma, and recovery can be lengthy. If you feel lost, the advice provided here may help you get started on the path to recovery.

1.Accept and embrace the abuse

Accepting that you were abused by a coworker, close relative, spouse or partner is an essential first step on the road to recovery. In the early stages of the healing process, you may find it difficult to set aside your justifications and defences for the other person's actions. You may even be willing to accept responsibility for your own actions if it prevents you from having to admit that a loved one intentionally harmed you. You might feel somewhat protected by denial. For many people, intense familial or emotional closeness overshadows reality. Accepting the fact that some people appear to care little about harming others is also challenging.

However, rejecting what occurred impedes your ability to deal with it and move on. Additionally, it can increase the likelihood that you will experience future pain. If you are aware that your loved one has experienced emotional suffering, you may wish to give them a second chance because you can relate to their situation.

Although compassion is always the proper response, mental illness never justifies cruelty. You may always assist them in seeking aid while allowing yourself sufficient space to do so.

Chapter 2: Clarify And Set Your Own Boundaries.

When possible, therapists and experts in the healing from abuse advise ending all communication with an ex-partner following the end of a relationship. It's not just a boundary they should avoid touching. You may initially find it quite difficult, but it is also a barrier for you. It is normal to feel compelled to call or respond to text messages and phone calls, especially if the person calling or texting apologizes and promises to improve. You can combat this temptation by limiting their contact information, email, and social media accounts. Because you never know when they may attempt to contact you in another way, it may be beneficial to have a plan for handling this situation.

Chapter 3: Acknowledge Your Irritation When Dealing With Narcissism.

Adjust the tone: The narcissist began the conversation about a past incident by attacking me personally. This blame strategy is intended to divert attention away from the actual displeasure, anxiety, or uncertainty. Because ignoring it is likely to result in additional conflict, I decided to accept a small task. Instead of taking it personally or assigning blame, I used empathy to create a different atmosphere. This halted the narcissist's momentum and provided me with a brief opening to ask a question.

Focus on the here and now. What caused this entire situation? Instead of continuing to discuss the past, I asked that we move on to the present. This was likely the main topic of our conversation, as the narcissist described the current state of affairs before expressing extreme discontent. Again, I was the target of multiple accusations, but this time I decided to acknowledge that their anger was justified. You are correct that it allowed me to be on their side as opposed to opposing them, and I am also disappointed by this.

Determine the insecurity by listening. Every narcissistic outburst masks an underlying insecurity, such as a fear of being abandoned, feeling inadequate, or being ignorant. Imagine it as a buried treasure that should not be displayed after being discovered. To reveal a narcissist's insecurities is tantamount to mutiny, and you will almost certainly receive a harsh response. Instead, acknowledge and address the existing unease without naming it. It is possible to acknowledge the uncertainty without revealing the narcissist's weakness by stating something along the lines of, "I can see how not knowing this information could make you sad."

Time to move ahead: This is the most challenging step. If done incorrectly or too soon, the conversation will begin again at step one. Timing is paramount. Before recommending a future joint action, allow the revelation to sink in for a moment. By including everyone in the plan's responsibilities, I address the underlying fear of abandonment. Instead of acting alone, narcissists seek assurance that they will be supported by a group. Moreover, this demonstrates their desire to command attention. This is an extremely potent usage of the term.

Now that I understand your perspective, we can proceed. This assertion should be followed by a few suggestions for moving forward with several alternatives. Too many options may increase frustration rather than decrease it. The lack of alternatives impedes the narcissist's ability to control the future.

If you're ahead, quit. Once a compromise has been reached, the discussion should conclude. Do not change the subject or attempt to justify why the initial assault was unjust. This will backfire and undo all of your prior accomplishments. It is preferable to wait some time before addressing new problems.

The Nature of Narcissistic Rage

Psychotherapist Heinz Kohut coined the term narcissistic fury in the 1970s to describe a narcissist's rapid and violent outburst, which may involve anger, hostility, and violence.

1 The behaviour occurs when a narcissist receives negative feedback that makes them extremely uncomfortable and activates their defensive systems. The rage caused by narcissistic injury may range from a minor annoyance to an outright physical assault. Certain narcissists may engage in verbal abuse, gaslighting, deflection, projection, or collapse. Depending on the severity of the injuries, others could act violently aggressively, which could be quite risky.

After taking their medication, narcissists will become emotionally, mentally, physically, or verbally aggressive. They respond in this manner because they are aware that they are being directly exposed and their true identity may be revealed. Narcissists "blow up" to divert attention away from the real issue and conceal who they are.

Frequent Responses to Offense and Narcissistic Fury

A narcissist may experience feelings of rejection or ridicule in response to the tiniest disagreement or critical remark, far exceeding the average threshold for offence. The first line of defense could consist of venomous yelling, screams, and absurd accusations. They could project their thoughts and feelings about themselves onto you.

Chapter 4: Several Types Of Narcissists

Although narcissists share many characteristics, they typically fall into one of three categories. They may be obvious, hidden, or toxic. These narcissists still meet the diagnostic criteria for narcissism, but exhibit distinct patterns of behaviour. The overt are typically quite exceptional, whereas the covert chose to conceal their narcissistic tendencies. Toxic narcissists are by far the exceptions who intend to inflict as much pain and suffering as possible for the sole purpose of causing others pain. Understanding how narcissists can present differently can make it easier to identify narcissists, as you will be able to recognise specific behavioural patterns. You will have a broader understanding of how narcissists can behave, making you better equipped to deal with them as they manifest.

The Disguised Narcissist

Covert narcissists, also known as vulnerable narcissists, conceal their manipulation strategies. They prefer to hide behind the victim mask because they are already highly sensitive to rejection and abandonment. They are motivated by their fear of rejection to guilt others into keeping them close, and the easiest way to do this is to pretend they need more assistance and support than they are receiving. People are more likely to assist those who are in pain or who have been victimised; therefore, the covert narcissist has a tendency toward victimhood.

Depending on recent events, the covert narcissist frequently oscillates between feelings of inferiority and superiority. When inferior, they seek out narcissistic supply by playing the victim to obtain what they require or desire. Once their egos have been bolstered by another person's attention, they are able to regain a sense of superiority.

Typically, covert narcissists are quite reactive. They do not cope well with the unexpected, and when they are denied what they were seeking, they have a tendency to explode, despite the fact that they typically present as timid, quiet, and the victim. When provoked, it becomes evident that the covert narcissist is a force to be reckoned with and can be incredibly violent and aggressive. They may prefer to portray themselves as victims in every circumstance, but they struggle to maintain this facade when they feel overwhelmed, revealing their true, vulnerable, raw, authentic self.

Typically, when confronted, a covert narcissist will resort to passive aggression in an attempt to maintain victimhood. The covert narcissist will maintain this persona if at all possible. Suppose, for instance, that your spouse is covertly narcissistic and frequently returns home from work late, leaving you scrambling to get to work on time because she leaves you alone with the children. In this case, you may suggest that she contact you if she believes she will be late so that you can plan accordingly and arrange for alternative care if necessary. Your narcissistic partner may begin to cry about how you do not trust her and how hard she is working for the family. She becomes so preoccupied with work and attempting to earn extra money that she forgets and is unable to be a viable partner.

Suddenly, the responsibility is transferred to you. You must either tell her that she is not stupid, thereby validating her victim mentality, or refuse to accept it and risk inciting her narcissistic rage. As is typically the case with narcissists, neither of the alternatives is particularly appealing to you. The only viable strategy is to not play at all.

The covert narcissist is ultimately quite fragile and self-conscious. She pretends not to be self-conscious because she is so preoccupied with it. This is the person she creates, her false self. She is essentially overcompensating for her flaws and creating something grandiose to make it appear as though she is significantly more self-confident than she actually is.

She makes her self-worth dependent on other people validating her, despite the fact that her inability to empathise effectively hinders her ability to form meaningful relationships. For her self-esteem to increase, she must feel wanted and needed by others; therefore, she pretends to be someone she is not. She attempts to establish rapport with others, preferring that her manipulation techniques go unnoticed in order to persuade them to like her.

Typically, the covert narcissist is the result of a childhood trauma that left her feeling abandoned or neglected. Creating a persona of perfection allows her to deny that the abuse, neglect, or abandonment, or whatever other trauma she endured, was not her fault and cannot be attributed to her.

While the grandiose narcissist seeks to be the centre of attention and seen as superior to all, gaining power and fame, the vulnerable narcissist's goals are significantly more reasonable.

She aspires to be the best in whatever position she occupies and a person whom everyone respects. She does not require supreme authority to be recognised for the effort she puts into her work. She prefers to be regarded as a great mother, wife, friend, and general member of the community over a leader. She will do whatever it takes to attain that position, including acting in ways that may not appear selfless, especially if others are present. She will behave generously, but only when there are numerous others present. She will act kindly toward others and sincerely attempt to make and maintain friendships, but her lack of empathy for others and constant attempts to cast herself as the victim will make it difficult to maintain relationships with her.

Chapter 5: How To Address Narcissistic Personality Disorder

You have options if you believe you have Narcissistic Personality Disorder. You have the opportunity and capability to take charge of your life and effectively manage this pervasive disorder, despite the difficulty involved. There are actions you can take to aid yourself and those around you. By engaging in these activities and accepting personal responsibility, you can enhance your life.

You must first recognise and accept that you have a problem with how you interact with the world. Once you recognise that you have a narcissistic personality, you can attempt to behave in a more socially acceptable manner. It is essential to know precisely who you are and how you act.

To accomplish this, you should compose a list of the maladaptive, destructive, and self-defeating behaviours you engage in. Admit which behaviours are causing you the most trouble. Then, create a second list of the behaviours you engage in that are constructive and beneficial, or productive. You should strive to engage in more of the second list of behaviours and avoid the behaviours on the first list.

Next, you must be willing to punish yourself when you engage in the first list of undesirable behaviours. How can you prevent yourself from engaging in these behaviours? When you find yourself engaging in the undesirable behaviours, you must be willing to perform these tasks.

Create a list of positive incentives or rewards for engaging in the adaptive behaviours. Give yourself a reward from your second list if you behave in an acceptable and appropriate manner. Positive and negative reinforcement teach individuals what is and is not acceptable behaviour. If you are willing to modify your behaviour, you can do so by recognising your behavioural responses and adjusting your actions accordingly.

The key is to consistently administer negative reinforcers and positive rewards when certain behaviours are exhibited. You must do it consistently. To administer such punishments and rewards, you must be willing to look at your behaviour objectively. If you are able to do so, you will be able to reduce the frequency of your problem and behaviours and encourage yourself to engage in the positive ones. These activities may be performed independently or under the supervision of a therapist. Any loved one in your life may be willing to assist you in modifying your behaviour in this manner. A therapist can be of great assistance in determining which behaviours are problematic and which are not, as well as in developing positive and negative reinforcers.

These may be challenging steps to follow. However, once you acknowledge you have a problem and are willing to monitor your behaviour, you can make significant life changes. You will get along with others better, and your life will become easier. However, you cannot relax your guard. Unfortunately, there is no cure for pervasive NPD. You can, however, control your behaviours and live a much better life through diligence.

Your NPD can be managed in conjunction with therapy and possibly medication to treat comorbid psychiatric symptoms. For instance, if your illness is accompanied by anxiety, you can take anti-anxiety medications to manage it. Take heart in the fact that you control your own destiny. You can choose to take positive actions to improve your life.

Chapter 6: Type-Casting The Darkness

You may have met multiple narcissists and concluded that they are all self-centered and lack empathy; however, not all narcissists are identical. To be able to deal with them more effectively, you must understand the two distinct types of narcissists: those who are grandiose and those who are vulnerable. Although both types of narcissists share certain characteristics, such as a sense of entitlement, a preoccupation with oneself, and a lack of empathy for others, they differ in a number of significant ways. While a grandiose narcissist has an inflated self-image, pretentiousness, an exaggerated sense of superiority, arrogance, a propensity to exploit others for their own benefit, and a desire for admiration, a vulnerable narcissist is typically defensive, insecure, shame-prone, hypersensitive, angry, hostile, lonely, and has low self-esteem.

So, is one type superior to the other, or should we state that one is more hazardous? Since grandiosity is readily apparent while vulnerability is concealed, grandiosity appears to be more admirable (at least on the surface) than vulnerability. Nevertheless, there is more to it. A narcissist with grandiose traits is more adamant about staying true to themselves and not accommodating others in any circumstance. The only type of narcissism that offers any hope or likelihood of change or improvement is the vulnerable type. A person with vulnerable characteristics may consider therapy and counselling because their desire to dominate others may be less intense. Both personality types, however, are problematic in their relationships. Living with a narcissist is unpleasant and dangerous. Consequently, it is prudent to comprehend the nuances of their characteristics.

Before delving deeper into grandiose and vulnerable narcissism, let's examine the five-factor model (FFM), which is applicable to virtually all types of people to varying degrees. When a person consistently displays a certain type of personality, it tends to shape their self-perceptions, characteristics, and values, as well as the expectations of those around them. The big five-factor model can also be used to predict an individual's response to people in general, as well as to all types of problems and stressful situations. Multiple personality and trait theories are combined to determine the causes and conclusion of narcissistic characteristics and NPD.

Now, all types of narcissists possess the aforementioned characteristics (to varying degrees), with the exception of "agreeableness," because the essence of narcissism is disagreeing with others. A narcissist may be an extrovert who enjoys meeting new people and has strong opinions and assertiveness. However, when these characteristics are accompanied by pride, selfishness, and insensitivity, a grandiose narcissist comes to mind. On the other hand, an introvert who prefers solitude may be considered a vulnerable narcissist if they enjoy seeking attention for who they are and appear to blame the world for their problems.

A grandiose narcissist is more likely to possess extraversion, openness, and conscientiousness, whereas a vulnerable narcissist will have a higher level of neuroticism. A vulnerable form of narcissism is deficient in all personality traits besides intelligence. Grandiose narcissism is characterised by an inclination toward more socially acceptable and positive traits, a high level of well-being, and presumed stability. In contrast, vulnerable narcissism is socially unfavourable, maladaptive, and predominantly depressed. Even though they are polar opposites, both types of personalities are challenging to live with. They are unsuitable for romantic relationships because neither of the two types is sensitive to the needs of others.

A victim of abuse must have a comprehensive understanding of narcissistic personality types in order to deal with them. By understanding the characteristics of their abuser, the victim can mentally prepare for the type of behaviour and relationship that may be in store. Their mind and body can prepare for confrontation through the use of anticipation. The victim will not be shocked by the bad behaviour, will be able to deal with it calmly, and will even be protected from future assaults.

Chapter 7: Cognitive Dissonance

Something that occurred between Aidan and his father when he was two shaped my parenting for years to come. In our bedroom one evening, I was folding laundry while Aidan jumped on the bed. Marty was in his office down the hallway. Aidan was winding up and becoming rowdy, as he typically did when he was tired, rather than winding down and falling asleep.

"Okay, Peanutty," I said, "I need you to calm down so that when I'm finished with the laundry, we can cuddle in your bed and I'll read you a story." I was exhausted after a long day, but I did not become angry with him. I allowed him to continue jumping while reminding him that he would soon have to stop. I did not anticipate him to calm down until I picked him up to change his diapers and put on his pyjamas.

I heard Marty slam his hands on the office desk and stomp down the hallway to our room. He walked over to the bed, grabbed Aidan by the shoulders, lifted him, yelled "Fuck!" while his face was inches from Aidan's, and then tossed him back onto the bed.

I was awestruck. I immediately dove under Marty's arms in order to go around him and pick up Aidan. He was in shock but had not yet started crying. I desired to change the scene as quickly as possible in the hopes that Aidan would forget what had occurred and that it would not be permanently imprinted on his mind. I hurriedly carried him to his room as he began to sob softly.

I gave him a moment to relax by saying, "Hey, honey, it's okay, Mommy's here, you're fine." As soon as he was comfortable in my arms, I picked him up, swung him around, and made aeroplane noises to make him laugh. I assisted him onto his changing table and gently tickled him to increase his laughter. I spent a half-hour changing him, snuggling with him on his futon, and reading the book Guess How Much I Love You by Sam McBratney after asking him what book he wanted me to read.

Once he was asleep, I quietly left his room and made my way to Marty's computer in the hallway. He did not stop what he was doing or acknowledge my presence when I entered the room.

"What the hell was that?" I inquired incredulously.

He asked, "What?" without ever looking away from the computer.

I stated, "What you just did to Aidan within the past thirty minutes." "I had planned to handle it. He was somewhat agitated, but he's only two! What do you anticipate?

Regardless, he stated, "I did nothing." He was intently focused on his computer, whatever he was doing.

"What?!" I said. "The poor child was in disbelief!"

He remained silent. He continued to type on the keyboard and stare at the monitor as though I were not present. I waited a few moments for acknowledgement, then turned on my heel, muttered "My God," and exited the room.

As I prepared for bed, my chest began to constrict as thoughts flooded my mind and questions I never wanted to consider began firing. Did he believe that if he didn't acknowledge his actions, I wouldn't notice? I understand he handles stress poorly, but wasn't that blatant child abuse? His conduct was so peculiar. I recalled the times when I was hospitalised or too ill to care for Aidan. I wondered what kind of stress my son would have caused him and what Marty would have done to silence him when no other adult was present. I pondered "shaken baby syndrome" and came to the conclusion that Aidan had not suffered from it. But what could have occurred, and what could I have done, if anything? What should I do next? Can I even conceive a second child with this man? Then I started to cry. I desperately desired another child. I desired another child more than anything else on earth. I told myself that Marty's anxiety is due to his new job and his efforts to earn more money through freelance graphic design. This was an isolated incident, and I'm sure Aidan is fine. In fact, by the time I tucked him into bed, he was laughing and completely himself. All will be well.

I worked diligently to persuade myself. Never again did I see Marty behave in this manner, but I never stopped feeling the need to protect my son from his father.

Aidan's learning difficulties were diagnosed as Attention Deficit Disorder as he grew older. As a teenager, he also developed anxiety and defiance issues that landed him in significant legal trouble. Could that have been explained by simple genetics? Or, could similar interactions with his father have had psychological or even physical consequences for his brain?

Despite the fact that I never again witnessed Marty's physical abuse of my son, Aidan informed me many years later that he had done the same thing—grabbed him by the shoulders and yelled in his face—on multiple occasions up until the time of the divorce. I believed confronting Marty that night would ensure he would never do it again, but it only ensured he would never do it in front of me again.

By 2003, I was consistently in good health. After nearly a year without colitis symptoms, I began to consider having a second child. I was committed to having at least one additional child. Since I had not witnessed another instance of abuse, I dismissed my concerns about Marty's parenting skills. I consulted Donna Marie, the Reiki Master/psychic who had assisted me with the timing of Aidan's conception, and I became pregnant with my second child on the first try with the IVF procedure.

Chapter 8: My Partner May Be A Narcissist.

Even with knowledge of the "official" diagnostic criteria, it is not always straightforward to identify a person with NPD, particularly if you are intimately acquainted with one. Typically, a qualified specialist must conduct a standard psychiatric interview to determine whether or not a person has NPD.

Nevertheless, being aware of the NPD symptoms may assist you in putting your relationship into perspective. Here are some warning signs and recommendations for how to respond.

Patients with NPD favour grandiosity and creativity. Initially, your relationship may have resembled something from a fairy tale. Within the first month, they may have showered you with compliments or professed their love for you.

Even if you just started dating, they may compliment your intelligence or emphasise your compatibility.

According to psychotherapist Jacklyn Krol, LCSW of Mind Rejuvenation

Therapy, narcissists enjoy bragging about their accomplishments and successes in a grandiose manner. They behave in this manner because they believe they are more intelligent and superior than everyone else, and because it gives them an air of confidence.

According to clinical psychologist Dr. Angela Grace, PhD, MEd, BFA, BEd, narcissists frequently embellish their skills and accomplishments in these narratives in order to gain others' admiration.

In addition, they are too preoccupied with themselves to pay attention to you.

According to Grace, there are two parts to this warning. Your partner won't stop talking about themselves and won't even initiate a conversation about you.

Consider these points: What happens when you talk about yourself? Do they make inquiries and demonstrate an interest in learning more about you? Or do they make everything about themselves?

Chapter 9: They Gain From Your Compliments.

People with NPD typically disagree with others frequently. If you investigate their connections further, you will discover that they do not have many close friends.

In addition, individuals with NPD may exhibit hypersensitivity and insecurity. If you wish to socialise with other individuals, they may become angry.

They may accuse you of not spending enough time with them, make you feel guilty for spending time with your friends, or criticise the types of friends you have.

They deceive you

Gaslighting, a defining characteristic of narcissism, is a form of emotional abuse and manipulation. In particular, in response to perceived challenges to authority or fear of desertion, people with NPD may tell outright lies, accuse others of error, twist the facts, and ultimately distort your perception of reality.

Chapter 10: What Is A Narcissistic Abuse Cycle & How Does It Work

The agony of being in a narcissistic relationship extends far beyond the question of what a healthy relationship looks like. It consumes you from the inside out to the point where you no longer recognise yourself. The destruction of a narcissistic abuse cycle is nourished by the guilt, shame, rage, and misery it causes.

Toxic is narcissistic or entitled behaviour. It dehumanises and degrades you to levels no human being should ever experience. Nevertheless, you can learn how to break the cycle of narcissistic abuse and liberate yourself. There is hope, and recovery from narcissistic abuse is possible.

What is the cycle of narcissistic abuse?

Without a healthy dose of narcissism, it would be impossible to get through that interview. Nonetheless, there is concern that narcissism is on the rise in this age of instant gratification and self-promotion.

It is essential to keep in mind that narcissism exists on a continuum, and that we are all somewhere on it.

Nevertheless, Narcissistic Personality Disorder is a distinct illness that is, thankfully, rare. However, it appears that specialists are divided over whether the prevalence of NPD is increasing.

Toxic individuals with narcissistic characteristics are, however, real and more prevalent than we would like. Moreover, if your parents were self-absorbed and exhibited narcissistic characteristics, you are more likely to fall into a narcissistic abuse cycle.

The cycle of narcissistic abuse is marked by ups and downs and cycles of hope and fear. A narcissist will confound and harm you through deception, grandiose gestures, and gaslighting. You will be torn between the desires to flee and remain.

The stages of the narcissist abuse cycle are idealise, devalue, and discard. They initially targeted you because they believe you can aid them and elevate their status. Then, they will lavish you with praise and elaborate plans.

You won't even realise you've been caught off guard, and you'll be completely unaware of all the invisible boundaries you've crossed that are buried beneath the avalanche of gifts.

In the second stage of the narcissistic cycle, they no longer value you. The actual emotional harm begins at this point. Eventually, if you're lucky, you'll be dumped in the final stage of the narcissistic abuse cycle.

Narcissistic personality disorder (NPD), also known as narcissism, is characterised by an exaggerated sense of self, unrealistic expectations of favourable treatment, and an extreme lack of empathy for others. People with narcissistic traits often struggle to maintain interpersonal relationships in all aspects of their lives, including at home, in the workplace, and in the community. Their relationships with others can at times be emotionally abusive.

3. The myth's original structure

The conception of Narcissus is preceded by a violent union: Kefiss took Liriope by force. It is structurally indicative of issues associated with the coniunctio archetype, the union of opposites. In clinical practise, it is well known that the treatment of narcissistic disorders has been primarily associated with exceptionally robust defences against relationships with others and the unconscious. This connection was thwarted by extreme dread ("Hands off! I do not require your hugs. I'd rather die than lie with you!" - a beautiful image of the narcissistic personality's attitude), so the healing therapeutic process focused primarily on the formation of unity in the transference-countertransference and on the ability to work with him. The myth of Narcissus and its explanations illustrate the coniunctio problem, particularly in those episodes involving Narcissus' echo and reflection.

But can we better understand the personality of Narcissus (whose myth serves as a figurative embodiment of the aetiology and potential transformation of clinical narcissistic disorder) if we begin our investigation by searching for the symbolic meaning of the violent scene, i.e., the violent connection that Narcissus' birth entailed? Perhaps we can learn something from Kephiss, the negative representation of masculine energy, or from Liriope's passive behaviour and her appeal to the seer Tiresias.

Consider first the image of Cefiss, the river god, who has a higher status and is more "archetypal" than Liriope, the nymph. It is evident that he is dominated and even overpowered by his masculine power, which Neumann referred to as the patriarchal ouroboros.

"The image of the patriarchal ouroboros approaches formlessness. It refers to the most fundamental archetypal conception of... the forces that exist within a woman and are intrinsically linked to her nature. This natural spirit, however, takes on a cosmic dimension. A more mundane interpretation may correspond to the image of an animal, such as a snake, bird, buffalo, or ram. As a demonic or divine spirit that takes root in a woman and impregnates her, however, he assumes the symbolic appearance of wind, storm, rain, thunder, and lightning... Despite its masculine-patriarchal aspect, the patriarchal ouroboros' symbolism transcends the polarity of sexual symbolism, uniting opposites into a single whole.

Cefiss is a river associated with the cult of Delphic Apollo94, and in relation to Apollo, it can be viewed as the spiritual excess exhibited by his temple's priestesses. In this instance, however, when we speak of violence against Liriope, we are referring to the negative aspect of the patriarchal ouroboros.

A Swedish story illustrates the connection between excessive masculine power and narcissistic behaviour. Jumping Elk and the Little Cottongrass Princess is the title:

Princess Cottongrass was infatuated with humanity: "I am young and delicate. I have enough kindness for everyone, and I wish to share it with all." She desired to leave the Castle of Dreams, where she and her parents resided.

Once upon a time, the princess encountered a Leaping Elk and begged him to take her away from the castle. In response, he cautioned her that this would be extremely difficult to accomplish, but Princess Cottongrass insisted, and he eventually agreed. The princess ascended the elk's back and departed from Dream Castle. Leaping Elk instructed her not to let go of his horns and not to converse with cunning elves who would attempt to confuse her. However, the treacherous elves began to question the princess about every aspect of existence. Princess Cottongrass let go of a hand that was supporting her as the crown began to slide off her head. The elves did exactly that: they seized the crown and fled immediately. The elk explained to the princess that she had never been so fortunate before. While the princess slept at night, he guarded her, "determined to fight and unwilling to be separated from her for any reason."

The following day, with the princess on his back, he rode through the forest as slowly as possible. When the forest witch began pestering the princess with questions, he reminded her not to let go of his horns. However, the princess' dress began to slip off her, and she attempted to grasp it. The witch then ripped the dress from the girl's hands and vanished from view. The elk reiterated to the princess that she was extremely fortunate, because if she had let go of both hands, the witch would have dragged her along with the dress.

This time, the moose became extremely enraged and chose to race without stopping. It became increasingly difficult for him to gallop aimlessly without knowing the path. Eventually, he brought the princess to a secluded lake. Leaping Elk cautioned the girl to protect the gold heart-shaped medallion she wore on her chest and to never allow it to fall into the water. However, when the overconfident princess looked into the lake, the golden heart her mother had given her fell into the water and she was unable to retrieve it. The girl pleaded with the moose to remain, but he insisted on leaving. The enchanted princess remained on the shore, continuing to observe the water and futilely search for her golden heart.

Numerous years later Princess Cottongrass is still seated on the shore, gazing in awe at the water that conceals her golden heart. She is no longer a young child today. It is now a slender plant that stands alone on the shore of a reservoir and is crowned with a white cotton95 flower.

In this story, the princess has a strong connection with her mother, symbolised by the golden heart she receives as a gift, but she is also extremely naive. She has a pronounced positive mother complex; she is like an infant living in a fantasy world. At the same time, she is aware that she must leave this world, which occurs, as is customary, under the influence of masculine energy, represented in the fable by the Leaping Elk. Eventually, the princess must pass through the narcissistic stage, in which the capacity to internally reflect the structure of the Self emerges and, as a result, identity formation occurs. This phase follows her separation from the castle's uroboric unity. The evil elves and the witch, conditioned by a negative maternal image, represent the regressive forces that seek to retain the princess. But, having gotten rid of the witch and the elves, she freezes by the pond, having lost the ability to continue along with the golden heart that her mother gave her, symbolising an erotic connection with the Self. Like Narcissus, she remains enchanted, regressively dissolved in the unconscious, and devoid of any possibility of a self-aware reflection.

As masculine energy is too primitive, uncontrollable, and intrusive, the original positive connection with the Self has been severed. The elk is a representation of the patriarchal ouroboros, a masculine force that lies deep within the individuation process that lifts a person out of unconscious life and its associated fusion and innocence. But the elk is too wild to be a suitable guide; it would be much better if the prince appeared and wed the princess, while the elk remained an observer from a distance and did not assume human form. In this instance, the development of femininity is impeded: the princess regresses and transforms into a plant, just as Echo does.

Excessive masculine force, exemplified by Kefiss and the elk, is a defining characteristic of the narcissistic state. Even with an initially positive maternal connection, the uncontrollability and excessively mixed needs of the patriarchal ouroboros render the original Self incapable of ongoing psychological development and identity formation. The attraction associated with masculine energy destroys femininity in both men and women, and in its place, compulsive behaviour takes over. (When you ask a narcissist who they are, they will typically tell you what they do.)

Chapter 11: Sexuality And Narcissism In The Shadows

Sexuality is an essential aspect of love, and narcissistic sexual behaviour poses numerous challenges to the relationship. And despite the fact that the atmosphere in "Fifty Shades of Gray" arouses the desires of many women, the reality of a romantic relationship with a narcissist destroys them beyond repair. The sexuality of narcissists is intense and incredibly intricate. Covert narcs have a propensity for perverse sex and compulsive and obsessive sexual behaviour. Obviously, everyone is entitled to his own sexual fantasies and behaviour, and there is nothing wrong with that so long as their execution is based on the conscious and voluntary consent of those involved and does not cause harm. In the case of covert narcissism, sexual behaviour becomes annoying or destroys the relationship. Consider the factors you must take into account if you fall into the trap of a covert narcissist.

Sexuality and narcissism in the shadows

Initial consideration should be given to covert narcissism from the perspective of human psychosexual development. A child's fascination with his body progresses through stages as he enters the world. Infancy marks the beginning of the oral phase, during which the child remains passive. Between the ages of one and three, he experiences the so-called anal phase, during which he enjoys feeling the anus and learns to control the excretion process. The so-called phallic phase occurs between the third and fifth years of life, when the child becomes interested in his external genitalia. Masturbation may then occur, and the successful completion of this phase leads to the inhibition of early sexuality and the onset of the next phase, the so-called phase of latency. Then, between the ages of 6 and adulthood, a person focuses on acquiring skills, including social skills required for interpersonal relationships. Beginning at the onset of puberty is the so-called genital phase, during which the adolescent derives pleasure from stimulating the reproductive organs.

From the perspective of the development of narcissism, the so-called Oedipus complex during the phallic phase is an important moment. The boy recognises his gender and adheres to social norms. Incorrect passage through the Oedipus complex leaves many traces on the personality and influences psychosexual development, including a fear of women. As a result of the difficulty of entering the phase of the Oedipus Complex, a perverse psychosexual structure develops. As a result of the desire for penetration, destructive tendencies or fantasies are triggered. Important at this stage is the father, who, if absent, cold, distant, or violent, prevents the boy from passing through the Oedipus Complex correctly. Also, the mother's role is not insignificant, as perverse individuals were unable to complete the separation process and establish a separate identity, including gender identity, during childhood. The consequence is a denial of the gender gap and the development of defences against dependence. A boy who experiences difficulties during the phallic phase of development due to the Oedipus Complex (this is known as fixation) will not enter the next phase of development, the period of latency, as it should. Important because the latency phase precedes later, more mature sexuality, preventing it from becoming perverted. A fixation on the phallic period shapes perverse sexual preferences and a propensity to repeat the emotional difficulties that accompanied disruptions in the passage of the Oedipus Complex. This includes the inappropriate formation of the superego and bisexual conflicts, which manifest in the adult's emotional and sexual life.

The sexual drive, or libido, turns inward, at which point the ego becomes a sexual object. In addition, at some point in their development, children experience a sense of omnipotence and greatness.

According to the principle that governs human psychosexual development, the defining moment is when a child realises his own individuality (as a separate person from his parents) and dependence on others. Due to the impossibility of establishing a healthy identity and autonomy in the covert narc's family, the child did not abandon the false belief in his own omnipotence. During this period, he experienced a narcissistic trauma that destroyed his sense of self-worth by emphasising his weaknesses and limitations. In self-defense, he directs his instincts toward himself. Not only libido (i.e., interest, curiosity) but also aggression is transferred to the self, resulting in extreme fluctuations in well-being ranging from self-omnipotence to inferiority and narcissistic depression.

When a narc's libido is not directed outward, others lose their perception of reality in his or her eyes. Relationships with them lose significance for many narcissists, for whom they resemble characters from a film or computer game.

Autoeroticism is a prominent aspect of the sexuality of the covert narc. It refers to more than just masturbation, but let's start there. When a covert narc masturbates, he makes love to himself; his fantasies are intricate and centre on a false image of himself. Because these fantasies are object-oriented, he employs fetishes in sexual rituals. Consequently, the propensity for paraphilic behaviours, such as fetishism or transvestitism, exists (dressing up, among others, to enhance the excitement and sensation). The covert narc typically develops an addiction to masturbation and pornography, which, as instrumental sex that separates sexual excitement from emotional intimacy, strengthens his focus on the object. Autoeroticism is manifested most prominently in covert narcissism by the fact that, while having sex with another person, the covert narc makes love to himself. In other words, the covert narc's libido is directed toward himself, or the false "I" ideal. When engaging in sexual activity with a narc, the partner becomes the object of the narc's masturbation. A person's body is the only tool necessary for autoerotic fantasy expression devoid of empathy. In psychology, dehumanisation is viewed as a defence mechanism that causes others to be treated indifferently. This permits the expression of hostility, aggression, and humiliation, as well as the exploitation of others for the narc's own benefit.

Dehumanization of others also protects the covert narc from the emotional stimulation caused by the perception of a real human emotion, which could be overwhelming for a covert narc. The dehumanisation of sexual partners by a covert narcissist is comparable to the dehumanisation of others by soldiers during battle, which enables them to kill their opponents.

Consequently, covert narcissism resembles the PTSD post-traumatic stress disorder typical of former frontline soldiers.

As a specific defensive mechanism, the covert narc uses sex. Narcissism is caused by childhood trauma, as a result of which the individual suffers mentally. The correction for narcissistic trauma/injury or painful childhood experiences is to transform them into positive emotions within sexual fantasies. The dehumanisation of the sexual partner into an object leads to perversion or paraphilias. As a result of these fantasies, the narrator feels triumphant and powerful, in contrast to the feelings experienced in childhood. Covert narcissism is linked to perverse sexual behaviour and paraphilias (sexual preference disorder). As a type of defence mechanism, kinkish and paraphilic tendencies of covert narcissism are sometimes explained (so-called sexualized reversal in the opposite direction). It transforms a narc's anxiety and depression into excitement and pleasure. Sexual pleasure temporarily dulls mental suffering, but does not cure it. Because the covert narc's current level of activity is no longer sufficient, the number of sexual stimuli increases.

Chronic boredom is associated with the trait of covert narcissism. There is a need to fill the inner void with powerful and novel stimuli. In turn, the anti-social aspect of narcissism is associated with a tendency to dominate, seek new sensations, and engage in risky behaviour. During his childhood with his parents or a parent whose covert narc feared and was never certain of the reaction he would receive, he unconsciously associated the pleasure of intimacy with danger, adrenaline, and disappointment. In the bedroom, he seeks excitement, danger, the unexpected, and forbidden / incompatible with social norms / immoral situations. Ge engages in multiple relationships simultaneously or sequentially, separating herself from other sexual objects from which she draws vital energy. He has sex with anonymous partners without attempting to meet them; he engages in orgies; he engages in paid sex; he demonstrates dominance and power; he uses utensils that heighten the intensity of sensations; and he engages in permissive practises for the dehumanisation of the sexual partner, objectification, robbing him of typical human features. He frequently utilises psychoactive or psychedelic substances to heighten his experiences. They give him more power and a higher state of consciousness, but they also help to dehumanise another person, expose the other person, and deprive the other person of free will, making it easier to treat that person as an object. The covert narc violates subsequent boundaries to satisfy his sexual urges. He derives his power from demonstrating his sexual prowess with numerous partners who resemble sexual devices or inflatable dolls. He has a pathological obsession with feeding his eternally hungry ego in order to strengthen his false self. He disregards sexually transmitted diseases because, when he is healthy, he feels omnipotent and invincible. Because he does not accept responsibility for his actions and their effects on others, he does not care whether he infects other sexual partners.

Chapter 12: Can Narcissistic Individuals "Catch" Yawns?

People typically yawn when they are tired or experiencing stress. Some individuals believe that narcissism can be determined by observing whether another person yawns when you do. The contagious yawn phenomenon may be related to mirror neurons, which are believed to play a role in empathy, according to experts. Imitating someone's body language can aid in establishing a strong connection and fostering a better rapport. This natural social response enhances your ability to comprehend others. People with less empathy may not be able to interpret body language as well. People with colder hearts were less likely to yawn when others yawned. Some may argue that narcissism and psychopathy are synonymous, but empathy appears to be the determining factor. The authors of the study reported that the reduced likelihood of yawning is not a complete inability to yawn. There are both individuals with low empathy and individuals with narcissism.

Chapter 13: This Behavior Stems From Their Own Insecurities.

Individuals with narcissism need to be in charge of everyone they interact with and every circumstance they find themselves in. Due to their lack of a personal value system, they adopt a set of values that will benefit them in their current circumstance.

Therefore, they decide to do whatever is necessary to obtain what they desire.

They are not required to believe that it is the right course of action; rather, it must produce the desired results.

This makes the Narcissist inherently untrustworthy, as nobody can predict what they will choose to believe in the face of constantly shifting circumstances.

Narcissistic individuals lack trust in others because they are aware that they are not trustworthy.

Consequently, they must ensure that they are not discovered or suffer a loss. The only way to accomplish this is to ensure that they maintain complete control at all times.

What they desire drives their behaviour. The action is not evaluated to determine whether it is right or wrong. As long as the action achieves what the narcissistic individual desires, it is, in their view, the correct action.

Similar to people who only apologise to calm a situation. They do not believe that they did anything wrong, but they feel compelled to apologise in order to influence the other party's behaviour.

In essence, it becomes a situation in which people do not act according to their own beliefs or the truth, but rather in a way that benefits them if they can convince others that they hold a particular belief. Whether or not it is true is once again irrelevant. The only thing that matters is the result, whatever the means.

Narcissistic individuals fall ill at the drop of a hat, for instance, when being ill and, as a result, eliciting pity seems to be the only way to garner all the attention.

Frequently, this occurs after an outburst of anger that did not produce the desired effect. Taking charge therefore not by dictating but by manipulating all situations by any means necessary. The narcissist is perpetually in pursuit of power. They manipulate their way into positions where they can secure this power in order to be able to use it if necessary.

They will always assert that they have no intention of harming you, but will always ensure that they have the means to do so.

By being made aware of the Narcissist's vindictive nature, all other individuals are put in a position where they know they will be attacked if they do not comply with his or her demands.

As a result, the narcissist exercises complete control over everyone.

People reach a point where they would rather self-mutilate than oppose a Narcissist with the ability to cause severe bodily harm.

Narcissists are not in the same category as the majority of people, who have no intention of harming others. They frequently state that they did not intend to cause harm, but that it was unavoidable. However, despite the fact that it wasn't required and was only optional, they did it anyway.

This control is extensive. To the extent that you will frequently find yourself being manipulated to make decisions on the Narcissist's behalf. These are typically unpopular decisions that the narcissist does not wish to make because they would reflect poorly on them. It then becomes necessary for them to ask you to make the decision on their behalf. This, so that you can appear to be the perpetrator and they can once again play the victim in the eyes of society, while obtaining precisely what they desired the entire time. While maintaining their own position, they throw you to the sharks. All is a game of control, both of people and of circumstances.

www.ingramcontent.com/pod-product-compliance
Lightning Source LLC
Chambersburg PA
CBHW070324120526
44590CB00017B/2813